LUCY BOSTON

LUCY BOSTON

Lucy Boston

Jasper Rose

A WALCK MONOGRAPH
GENERAL EDITOR: KATHLEEN LINES

HENRY Z. WALCK, INCORPORATED
NEW YORK

For E.V.

Library of Congress Catalog Card Number: 66-11118
© Jasper Rose 1965
First American Edition 1966
Printed in Great Britain

CONTENTS

A Note about the Author

Jasper Rose is a historian and painter. He has taught history at Keele and at Cambridge (where he held a fellowship at King's College and was a University Proctor). After a spell of two years at Rice University, Texas, teaching oil painting and art history he joined the faculty of the new campus of the University of California at Santa Cruz in the autumn of 1965.

As a child he did not enjoy children's books. With a few very important exceptions he still prefers those written for grown-ups. But then, as a child, he did not much care for rice pudding or junket or Turkish delight. He still doesn't.

I. Yew Hall

There is something incongruous and comical in the fact that Swinburne—not the reformed Swinburne, carefully nannied by Watts-Dunton, doled out his daily portion of bottled beer, who is so brilliantly portrayed by Max Beerbohm in his essay *Number Two the Pines*, but the unregenerate Swinburne, drunkard, masochist, dabbler in and scribbler of erotica—should have been one of the warmest defenders of Dr Thomas Bowdler's castration of the plays of Shakespeare. But his reason for defending the bowdlerising of Shakespeare was both sound and revealing: Bowdler had made Shakespeare accessible to Victorian children—and this was a good thing.

Today, the idea that Shakespeare should be tampered with in order to protect the innocence of children seems slightly ridiculous; we take it for granted that in so far as children are innocent, they will simply skim over the many indecencies scattered in all his plays, probably without noticing them, and certainly without taking harm from them —an assumption that is on the whole legitimate. Yet the essence of his argument is surely right. Children, as well as grown-ups, enjoy good writing, great writing; indeed, they often enjoy the same literature. The point needs making now—perhaps it needed making just as strongly then. For the High Victorian period saw not only striking and mawkish developments in the romantic mythology of childhood, but also an immense boom in the publication of a specialised literature aimed at children. The roots of children's books as a separate literary form lie in the latter half of the eighteenth century; the works of Mrs Trimmer, and such popular successors as Anne and Jane Taylor and Mrs Sherwood hardly suggested that a great destiny was in store for it; much of the torrent of children's books that poured from the presses in the second half of the century, though very pretty when illustrated by Arthur Hughes or Kate Greenaway, was, considered as literature, poor—sentimental, jejune and crude. Indeed, until today, it seems to have been the aim of a great many professional writers of children's books to serve up something that resembles a marshmallow, squashy, sickly, sticky, over-sweet and pink-and-white. Increasingly commercialised attempts to pin down a market—usually in terms of age groups—have not helped; they have encouraged authors both to talk down to children and to adjust their stories too nicely to what they suppose to be the mental horizons of their audience: as a result children are often offered books which are precisely calculated *not* to give a jolt to their imaginations, or to stimulate their aesthetic feeling, or even to extend their vocabularies.

This is not to deny that children are different from adults. Nor is it to assert that the children's book is necessarily a bastard literary form. Rather it is to emphasise that most children's books do not attempt to be literature, and that to write a really good book for children demands great literary skill. It is significant that the few classics of children's literature have mostly been written by people whose

main claim to literary fame lies elsewhere—
Thackeray, Kipling, Walter de la Mare, Hilaire
Belloc, for instance. It is also significant, but not
surprising, that books like *The Rose and the Ring*
and *Alice in Wonderland* exert as much fascination
on adults as they do on children: they owe their
status as classics not so much to the fact that they
are outstanding children's books, but to the vivacity
of their ideas, and the artistry with which they are
written. To say that a book is 'for children of all
ages' hardly conjures up an attractive vision of its
audience: toothless ancients, mouths forever cack-
ling, eyes forever watering; hearty middle-aged
gents, fat back-slappers, ceaselessly executing hops,
skips and jumps, wreathed in rosy dimples; young
men and women who still take teddy bears to bed
every night. Nor is it any better to turn the idea
upside down: nothing could be more repellent than
a book for 'adults of all ages'—imagine all those
owlish ten-year-olds turning down their mouths
and tutting, as they adjust their spectacles for the
next chapter. Yet there are books which have this
great width of appeal; however much they may be
about things which children in particular find interesting, perplexing, funny and exciting, they never
decline into the triviality and sentimentality that
grown-ups find boring, but rather enchant all
readers by elasticity of imagination and clarity of
style.

The bulk of Mrs Boston's published writings are,
in the cant term of booksellers, 'children's books'.
Without necessarily wishing to claim classic rank
for them, it seems best to insist from the outset that

though these books are about children and predomi-
nantly written for children, and though they find
in children their largest audience, they have this
width of appeal. It is not simply that they avoid the
faults common in many books that might otherwise,
through exciting plot, lively narration and charm of
style, please grown-ups: coarse psychology, cheap
and obvious moralising, garish, swashbuckling
improbability of incident. It is rather that beneath
the surface of stories which never flag in interest
and handle such easily exaggerated and flashy subjects as ghosts, giants, escaped gorillas and witches
with restraint and subtlety, Mrs Boston explores a
number of perennially interesting human predica-
ments—what it is like to be blind, what it is like to
have to withhold a tremendous secret from some-
one one deeply loves, what it is like to have to confront evil—and deals with themes of great serious-
ness, the most pervasive of which is the relationship
of the present to the past; that she portrays children, in particular their inner thoughts and the
freshness of their response to all sorts of experiences, from eating sandwiches or watching a down-
fall of snow to being attacked by an owl in a ruined
house or finding an ancient manuscript, with
accuracy, sympathy, impartiality and vividness—
they are as real, but not as horrifyingly precocious
as the children of Ivy Compton-Burnett; that,
above all, she has an ability to present things, land-
scapes, animals, houses, objects, people, with an
extraordinary concreteness, that she is a master
of phrase, of image, that she is a remarkable
writer.

The notion that people are 'born' writers, or musicians, or architects, or prime ministers, or parsons, or pop-singers, is not an easily tenable one. Think of George Moore's forty years' battle with words, or Cézanne's desperate struggle with paint. Yet it is tempting to use the phrase of Mrs Boston: her first book *Yew Hall* seems so polished, so effortless, so mature. As an author she appears to have sprung out of the ground fully armed.

But at a most unusual age. The history of literature furnishes very few examples of men or women who commence a serious and distinguished career as writers at the age of sixty. Sixty is an age when most poets and novelists are already dead. Sixty is an age when second-rate diplomats and braggart generals concoct their memoirs. Sixty is an age to start thinking of laying aside pens along with squash rackets, ping-pong bats and swords. It really is very surprising indeed that at sixty Mrs Boston should decide to take up *her* pen and wield it so actively and well.

Anyone who knows Mrs Boston, however, is prepared for surprises. There is something mysterious, bold, unexpected and dramatic about her very appearance. With her brown skin, quick worn hands, forcefully modelled head, strong nose and jet black hair she might be taken for one of Borrow's gipsies—in fact she had two Jewish great-grandmothers. Her face is dominated by her eyes, dark, large, jewel-like, ready to gleam, swivel or smoulder on the least provocation, and a pair of incredibly agile eyebrows—almost as furry as Kipling's—which seem capable of transforming themselves into a whole flock of rooks, and lend her sometimes a touch of comicality, sometimes a hint of ferocity —when she bends them on an unwelcome visitor, or an inappropriate remark. It is odd that though her face is so mobile and expressive, now very gay, now darkling and melancholy, it is difficult to gauge her underlying mood; ultimately an inscrutable, contradictory, redoubtable visage, requiring a Rembrandt to do it justice.

Like her face, her life has been full of surprises, sudden changes of course, breakings out in new directions. She was born in 1892 at Southport, Lancashire, into an intensely evangelical family; her father was an engineer with a passion for religion. He died when she was six and her chief memory of him is of daily family prayers when he would hold her between his knees and guide her fat finger along beneath the huge letters of the text of the day as he read in the family Bible. From her account he would appear to have been a boisterous, energetic man; her mother had none of his large religious dynamism and when he died the family atmosphere petered away into a meagre pietism which found expression in prohibitions against dancing and going to the theatre.

It was a strict and narrow upbringing. Company was curtailed to the family circle, lest the children should mix with the ungodly. Fortunately Mrs Boston was one of six children and found in her three brothers natural and obstreperous allies. She needed some for at sixteen she fell into religious doubts and forthrightly refused, in the face of great pressure, to be confirmed. At about this time—and it is a fact which reveals a great deal about her family circumstances—she was sent to a Quaker school in Surrey in order that her broad Lancashire accent should be rectified. It was not a completely successful operation!

Clearly Mrs Boston was a sensitive and self-aware child. At the age of ten she spent a year in a Westmorland village; she traces her lifelong love of the English countryside back to this time. When only eight she knew that the abiding passion of her life would be 'looking at living landscape'. Clearly, also, she was and has remained a counter-sug-gestible person. Her mother considered food un-interesting and wine a devilish invention. Mrs Boston is a splendid cook whose Christmas feasts remind one of the descriptions of Old Christmas in Washington Irving's *Bracebridge Hall*; and she commands her male guests to uncork the bottles with peculiarly gleeful relish. Maternal disapproval, it would appear, only egged her on to become an accomplished and indefatigable dancer; the latest evidence of her delight in the theatre is an unlimited, positively abandoned worship of Nureyev.

It might appear that Mrs Boston revolted com-pletely and successfully from the standards and point of view of her early environment. Yet though she seems both in her personality and her writing to bear no taint of religiosity, of puritanism, of that fear and contempt for beauty and the arts which characterised so many evangelical households throughout Victorian times, in many other ways, in her independence of mind, her close and penetrating observation of human motives and foibles, her capacity for clear, caustic, high-principled judgements, her thoroughness once she has launched herself on any undertaking, her confidence in her own conscience, she would appear to be indebted to that stringent, upright, limited but courageous culture. The evangelicals never lacked boldness in their loves and hates and admired nothing so much as energy of conscience.

In 1914, after a year in Paris being 'finished' and learning the language, Mrs Boston went up to Somerville, Oxford, taking her counter-suggestibility with her. Whether it was simply that she was rather older than the other girls of her year, or because the war immediately denuded Oxford of all passable young men, or because of her natural rebelliousness, she found the whole set-up intolerable: she describes the Somerville of her time with gusto as a dismal coagulation of formality, militant feminism and schoolgirl crushes, full of avidly ambitious young harpies and presided over by a sort of Gilbert and Sullivan headmistress whose social currency consisted of outsize snubs. She read Classics for a couple of terms, distinguished herself at Lacrosse, broke all the available rules, and gladly left for London to train as a nurse.

Nothing in her previous life, neither her home, nor her year in Paris, nor her sojourn at Oxford, nor her brief training at St Thomas's hospital (invaluable though it was), not even her own ebullient and refractory imagination, had prepared her for the French hospital to which she was posted. Perhaps like many other carefully nurtured young people she looked forward to casting gentilities aside and rubbing up against the real roughness and rawness of life. But she was profoundly shocked by the conditions she encountered: the more aristocratic French nurses left the more mutilated casualties to die, the less aristocratic French nurses made love to the less mutilated casualties, and only the English nurses did any work. The callousness and immorality and dishonest muddle were a terrible surprise. Yet with her natural resilience and energy Mrs Boston managed to fulfil her obligations, enjoy herself and find the whole experience most illuminating. The fact is that Mrs Boston has a strong streak of turbulence in her make-up. Even now she is torn between distress and exaltation when storms ravage the precious trees in her garden; and one of her yearly pleasures is a visit late in the autumn to the coasts of Cornwall to savour the violence of the weather and watch the titanic assault of waves on crag. The point is worth emphasis. For her delight in drama, her excitement at the naked display of temperament, form an important part of the stuff of her books. Critics have noticed the delicacy and tenderness in her writing; but she also revels in strong passions and loves to portray a piece of villainy. Fundamentally she has more taste for rats and snails and puppy dogs' tails than for sugar and spice.

During her marriage, which lasted from 1917 to the middle of the 1930s, Mrs Boston's unusual combination of zest, combativeness and sensitive aesthetic refinement found expression in comparatively conventional and commonplace activity. She and her husband lived in a beautiful Queen Anne house in Cheshire; from it she waged war on I.C.I.—on the pollution and poisoning of a particularly beautiful countryside by the waste products of chemical industries. Apparently her war was unavailing; she was powerless to prevent the creeping erosion of ugliness and the killing of trees and crops by gas.

Perhaps it was as much because she was disheartened by this losing struggle as by the turn her personal affairs had taken that she left England in 1935, intending never to return. Perhaps, too, it was partly because her direct efforts to save the living beauty of grass, leaves and flowers were frustrated that she began actively to pursue the arts. In the early 1930s she wrote a good deal of poetry—even though it does not, like the poetry of Thackeray's Miss Bunion 'breathe a withering passion, a smouldering despair which would melt the heart of a drayman were he to read it', it is strong stuff—but at this stage of her life she was really more seriously interested in painting and music. Readers of her books will not be surprised at the interest in painting: their many brilliant descriptive passages reveal not just a sharp eye for detail, but that real appreciation of shapes, forms and textures which only comes with serious practice of the art. She herself attributes her failure to persist with her painting to poor eyesight. Perhaps, too, the great gifts of her brother, James Wood, her son Peter, and her closest friend, Elizabeth Vellacott—

of whose immaculate and visionary drawings and paintings she has assembled a fine collection— made her misdoubt her own. It was probably a wise decision for the work that survives is accomplished but, with the exception of two candlelit interiors of King's College Chapel, lacking in the delicacy, wit and sensitivity of her writing. It suggests the boldness and vigour of her character, but not at all its complex sensibility.

Mrs Boston's life on the continent, frequenting the artists' studios and the galleries of Florence, listening with growing addiction to music in Vienna and Salzburg, was cut short by Mussolini and Hitler. She came back and settled in Cambridge at what was for her, personally, a lucky moment. In 1939 the Manor House at Hemingford Grey came on the market and she was able to buy it and set it in order just before the war started.

Since then the outward tenor of her life has been both very busy and very tranquil. During the war she ran a most successful music club in her house for members of the R.A.F. stationed on the fens. Since the war she has laboured at the task of developing her garden, planting it with many hundreds of varieties of roses—she allows the bushes to grow as large as trees—great banks of irises and thick bulwarks of bamboo. In the summer she toils and loiters among her flowers and birds all day.

It is a question where she gets so much energy. The garden is very large, but always in superb order. Always the house seems to sparkle. Always Mrs Boston seems to be entertaining. Always she seems to get to see all the most important shows in London. Always she is game for a party or a concert or theatre in Cambridge, and as keen and excitable as a child on such occasions. Even in the winter when she has fewer visitors, goes on fewer jaunts and can do little in the garden, she is tremendously busy and active, repairing the antique patchwork quilts she uses as curtains and steadily stitching new ones. It is typical of her unquenchable activity that when a few years ago her great Persian carpet wore into holes she set to and learnt how to make the correct knots and spent a whole winter standing at a bench several hours a day knotting up the holes.

The commodious and comfortable business of her life since the war only makes her sudden blossoming as a writer the more surprising. The explanation may be partly in the fact that in spite of her manifold activities she found the winters of a small village on the edge of the fens lonely; and partly that age brought with it release and repose from the more scorching commands of living, more freedom and certainty of mind with the mellowing of sheer physical vitality.

But there is one much more obvious factor which, as must be apparent to all her readers, has had a decisive influence on her writing, and is a key to explaining how and when she came to be a writer: her house. Yew Hall, the house which gives her first novel its title, Green Knowe and the house in which her unpublished novel, *Persephone*, comes to a finish, are all very close portraits of the Manor, Hemingford Grey. In a sense, as she indeed suggests of *Yew Hall*, this house is the central character, almost the hero of all the published books. Certainly it sustains them, a formidable yet poetic backbone of stone. In as much as any single thing inspired her to write, it was her house.

All her life Mrs Boston had known the Manor from the outside. But when she came eventually to buy it she could not know, though with an intense intuition she guessed, how very remarkable a house it was. Even externally its majestic, towering, gabled simplicity of shape was swathed in awkward excrescences; internally it was a mass of shoddy, decrepit, blaring, rickety flimflam which concealed completely its true nature; it was as though a goddess had been caparisoned in the clothes of a charlady going to a wedding. The garden was wilderness.

The stripping away of all the shoddy, from recent chromium-plated light fittings and purple ceilings to the sinister, windowless garrets reached by tunnels which necessitated groping in the dark on all fours (in which earlier occupants had kept some of the servants) to reveal the essential structure, the unblocking of Norman round-headed windows, the tearing away of plaster disguise from doorways which were Norman arches, the excavating of the immense Elizabethan fireplace in the dining room, must have been extraordinarily exciting—like striking the chains off an ancient king imprisoned for a lifetime. It was made more tense by the discovery that in places the walls, three feet thick, were being upheld by rotten three-inch planks, and the fact that the architect in charge of the restoration had passionately archaeologising tendencies (where a stone was missing from an arch, he wished to point the fact for posterity by filling in with brick). A long procession snaked about the house: the architect would proclaim to his assistant his honest but often stark intentions; the message would be relayed to the clerk of works, and in turn to the foreman, the head bricklayer, his assistant, and finally Mrs Boston at the tail—and her firm resistance, in the name of both beauty and comfort, retailed all the way back up the line. Through vigilance and indomitability, Mrs Boston triumphed and the old house re-emerged.

It is tempting to describe the house in detail—but unnecessary, for Mrs Boston has done it with both brilliance and fidelity in her books, particularly in *Yew Hall* and the first of the Green Knowe series, *The Children of Green Knowe*. Not only are the house and garden strikingly as she describes them, but so, too, is the furniture, from the wooden angels crowned by birds' nests and the mirror in the hall to the huge Chinese lantern and mysterious Persian mirror in the music room: the chief thing missing is the great statue of St Christopher, which plays such an important part in *The Children of Green Knowe*.

So I shall quote instead two passages from *Yew Hall* which not only evoke some of the quality of the house—and incidentally illustrate the thoughtful elegance of style in which the book is written—but more importantly suggest some of Mrs Boston's feeling for it. The first is part of the peroration of

her major account of the house and its history:
'I have called my house a barn, an ark, a ship, a
boulder, a wood . . . I believe that if . . . (it) were
magnified as big as the sea it would show as much
sparkle, as much rhythm and vitality, as much
passion as the sea. It is a natural thing, made out of
the true earth. The walls are three feet thick, not of
solid stone, but of quarried stone brought here by
barge and laid piece over piece with the grain
always lying as it lay in the cliff face, but here with
seams of air between the stone . . . They rest easily
on the earth and grow to the impressive height of
the roof-tree without force, not locked and rigid like
bricks and mortar, nor steelbound and plugged with
sterile composition. They breathe around me.
Sitting alone here for the longest series of wordless
winter nights I feel neither shut in nor shut off, but
rather like the heart inside living ribs.' The second
occurs a little later: 'As I turned to the house it lay
huge on the gravel like a ship in dock, larger than
life, its high pointed gable end as significant and
peculiar to itself as the features of a remarkable
face. Approximately fifty generations have lived in
those walls, not all of one family nor even of one
race. Saxons, Normans, Welsh, Irish and West-
countrymen, Crusaders, family rivals, hereditary
enemies, the ambitious and the reverent. Human
passions are limited in number and the same
situations recur for ever in varying intensity.
It seems reasonable to suppose that in such a
length of time some version of every possible
passion good and bad will have played itself out
here.'

23

Now, merely to peel off a few layers of wall-paper in a dingy Victorian villa provokes the imagination to conjure up the history of its past. Releasing, recreating her almost immemorial house, must have acted as a most potent catalyst on Mrs Boston's mind. The more she uncovered, not only of its physique but of its history, the more she learned of its moods, its underlying climate, the greater the kinship and affection she felt for it and the more her imagination fed on it. In the loneliness of those long wordless winter nights it must have seemed almost as though the walls spoke and dictated stories to her.

It may seem fanciful to attribute Mrs Boston's sudden eruption as a brilliant writer to her house. But that is partly because our civilisation is so makeshift, improvised, temporary, and so contemptuous and negligent about the power of particular places, that it has made us unwilling to recognise the spiritual strength of a physical environment. Yet almost all of the people who visit the Manor at Hemingford, are literally dumbfounded by the serenity of its beauty and antiquity. In some mysterious way Mrs Boston's spirit has been nourished, calmed and enlarged by her house, and in a sense all her books commemorate her debt to it.

Frankly, it is a magic house. Perhaps it is this, and the fact of its immense antiquity that led Mrs Boston to writing about and for children. For what more splendid setting could there be for children's stories? In what better way could the ancient dignity of the house be enlivened than by the cheerful, unboding friendliness of children? In what better way could a child's imaginative boldness and appreciation of age and mystery be provoked than by such a time-outlasting place?

II. Plotting

As E. M. Forster reminded his audience with arch reluctance in *Aspects of the Novel*, a novel has to tell a story. Of course a few novelists have succeeded in by-passing this crude requirement; and it is possible to saunter about the company of Laurence Sterne or Henry James without losing patience with their digressions, their dilatoriness, their lack of interest in arriving at a destination. But Sterne and James are acquired, sophisticated tastes. Most people, in particular young people, read a story in order to find out what happens: a dawdling tale does not appeal to them very much.

And yet who has not felt that sense of disappointment which comes at the end of a breakneck rush through a book that is fiercely driven by its plot, in which incident follows incident follows incident without a pause, when at last all the villains are finally discovered and delivered up to justice and all the heroes and heroines safely dead, or safely married and prepared to live happy ever after? The pages turn faster and faster, the print positively leaps up to meet the eye, as one hurries to the conclusion. A jolt (the hound of the Baskervilles bays his last, Umslopogaas crashes to the ground, the Iron Duke in person pins a medal to young Tommy's breast) and then—FINIS. It is a bit like travelling in a jet. One arrives far too soon, feeling dishevelled and hectic, and with the curious sensation of not having lived during the journey.

It is one of the most obvious, it is also one of the

most important, virtues of Mrs Boston as a writer that she has a fine sense of tempo. It is only very rarely, and in her earlier books, that she loses sight for a moment of the need to keep the story going; she judges the time to give a plot its head, to allow a torrent of events to sweep the book onward, with great finesse: she has the courage and ability to dawdle or to hurtle as the occasion demands. If one is to liken her books to any means of locomotion, it must be to a country train. They ramble through the countryside at an amiable speed, never disdaining a stop at an inviting sunny station—sometimes the guard and the ticket collector seem to have rather a lot to say to each other and one is left to watch the flight of butterflies in the white afternoon. Sometimes they clink to a halt in the midst of nowhere, gazed at by imperturbable cows. But there is always plenty to look at; one has every confidence that eventually one will reach journey's end; and, as the destination comes in sight, they always manage to put on a pretty turn of speed and rattle in with an impressive snort of steam and sparks flying. The earlier books took more circuitous routes and stopped at every tiny Halt; *A Stranger at Green Knowe* and *An Enemy at Green Knowe* have more powerful engines and travel more impatiently and directly.

Of course the image is inadequate; it is also perhaps a bit misleading. For there is nothing haphazard about the organisation of the books; and they do not simply transport the reader from point A to point B along a single track. Characteristically, Mrs Boston entwines a number of different themes to form her plot. At first reading one of these themes appears to dominate the whole structure of the book—largely because she usually manages to contrive a startling dramatic climax to it. But on re-reading and pondering the books, their centres of gravity seem to shift; relationships between characters at first unnoticed impose themselves with a different dominance, the mood and colour of the stories change. Like a Persian carpet or a patchwork quilt, one can read their patterns in many ways.

This complexity of design is perhaps most evident in *Yew Hall* (1954), her only 'grown-up' novel to be published. Initially one takes the main theme to be the relationships between Mark Howard, his wife, Arabella, and his twin brother, Roger. Their story, which in its starkness and violence might furnish the basic material for a Greek tragedy or a sensational novelette, can be quickly sketched. Arabella, sequestered in the country and bored, seduces Roger, much against his will and judgement. She then attempts to murder her husband. The attempt, which fails, is discovered by Roger, who promptly kills Arabella and commits suicide.

Mrs Boston handles this primary plot skilfully. Arabella is dedicated to her own beauty—typically one is shown her 'sitting with pictures of Paris fashions spread out round her, painting her nails'— and cannot resist the need to exercise its power, however contemptibly. Her husband—'a huge man, handsome like a statue in St Paul's'—is intelligent, magnanimous, monumentally trusting, a man of high military honour. Roger has as sharp a sense of honour and is much more perceptive; he can see the danger of his predicament—but cannot resist it, or forgive himself for succumbing to it. By successfully portraying Arabella as a mixture of sweetness and predatoriness, at once infantile, well-bred, exquisite and coarse, by giving a subtle emphasis to the brothers' warmth of feeling for each other, and by devising a particularly insidious means for Arabella's attempt at murder, Mrs Boston contrives to produce an exciting *finale* which manages to transcend the rather melodramatic turn of the story.

But this harsh story is only one, and ultimately the least interesting though most forceful dimension of the book. For the action takes place in an ancient house, and is recounted by the owner. It might appear that this woman simply takes the part of a chorus, interspersing the action with superb evocations of the house and of the changing seasons, and interpreting and commenting on the actions of the chief protagonists. But fairly quickly the reader comes to feel that her role is more like that of a *confidante* in a Racine tragedy, embroiled in the action itself, powerless to avert destiny, indeed, unwittingly involved in shaping the catastrophe. But even this understates the importance of the narrator. From her relationship with her tenants sprout many deftly-managed themes. The clearest of these is the sporadic and uneasy encounters between owner and tenants forced to share the same house; the way in which the narrator is slowly, magnetically drawn into the drama going on under her own roof is brilliantly done. This theme begets another, hinted at rather than explicit: a queer and intermittent jealousy develops between the narrator and Arabella; the older woman comes to judge the younger more and more severely but is at the same time enthralled by her; and while it is Arabella who seduces Roger, it is the narrator who falls in love with him. The narrator's feeling for Roger, dignified, measured but profound, emerges as the most moving human relationship in the book.

But there are other relationships equally important in sustaining the book's power. As we have seen, there are many passages devoted to descriptive panegyric of Yew Hall itself. An inattentive reader might see in these no more than an attempt to evoke the *genius loci*, relevant to the development of the story only in the most general sense. But the house is more than a foil to set off the action; it is more like a touchstone by which the motives of the actors are to be judged. The narrator certainly uses it as a test; she is intensely conscious of the reaction of her tenants to it. Roger's deep response to its spirit—when he first comes into the music room he says, perhaps a trifle hyperbolically, 'It's like sitting right inside Beethoven's skull'—both helps to create and exemplifies the bond between them. And part of the tension between the narrator and Arabella results from Arabella's desire to be queen of the house, and the narrator's consciousness that her beauty is no mean title to such an honour. Right at the end of the story Mrs Boston makes explicit the place of the house in the book, its function to beget, environ and chasten the drama in Mark's penultimate words: 'The thing about this house . . . is that it makes you see how just this kind of thing— I mean us, now—has been going on always, as far back as you can think. There's such a lot of time, when you try to get the idea of it. It goes on and on; like mountains. They are bigger than you could possibly imagine till you get off the beaten track— hung up somewhere. Then they put you in your place . . . And it's not such a small place either, it takes some filling.'

This brief analysis, though it reveals something of the structure of *Yew Hall*—the small triangle of relationships amongst the Howards themselves, embedded within a larger triangle of those between the Howards, the narrator and the house—hardly does justice to its complexity. It is a short book, but a very rich one. Structure and story apart, it is full of incidental pleasures to pause over, sharp social observations, as when Mrs Boston describes the costume of painters—'Both sexes were dressed as if their motives were to prompt paintings, as if it didn't matter what they actually looked like, the eyes of other painters could be relied upon to translate them into pictures'—tough dissection of human motive, and descriptions of nature which may be read as set pieces, complete in themselves.

It is almost as difficult to give an adequate account of the structure of Mrs Boston's children's books. Less densely interwoven than *Yew Hall* they are still full of crosscurrents and under-currents; and like it, they make the reader wish to saunter and hasten at the same time.

It is probably as well to start a discussion of these books by making a few elementary points. As their titles suggest, they form a loose series; all of them are about the mysterious and ancient house called Green Knowe and some of its present and past inhabitants. Like Trollope's two great sets of novels, the Barsetshire novels and the political novels, they are all fully independent and can stand on their own feet; but they do have a cumulative power and gain a good deal from being read in the order in which they were written and published. The interrelationships between them resemble more closely those between say, *The Prime Minister* and *The Duke's Children* than those between *Framley Parsonage* and *The Small House at Allington*: for most of them share the same cast of main characters as well as the same setting.

To call Green Knowe a 'setting' is, as I have already suggested, an understatement. In *The Children*, *The Chimneys* and *An Enemy* it stands right at the centre of the plot. Even in *The River* and *A Stranger* the characters never stray very far from its domain and the surprising events that take place in them are largely made credible by its ability to authenticate the exceptional and miraculous. Like the rabbit hole and the looking glass in *Alice*, in all the books it is the portal to another world in which human sensibilities are both enhanced and altered. Perhaps it is the house and the garden rather than the characters which impart to them that very distinctive flavour they have in common. It may be a naïve, but is also a deep pleasure to find old acquaintances and friends in a new book. Children—and grown-ups—tremble with anticipatory excitement when the massive gable of Green Knowe comes in sight again amongst its trees, and they step inside the hall with its clusters of vases full of roses, its wooden angels bearing birds' nests and confront themselves in the mystifying mirror at the far end.

The Green Knowe books also share a major similarity in their formal structure. All are built out of a number of adventurous episodes, each with its own dramatic turning point, which are yet bound into the total development of the story. In the first two books, *The Children* and *The Chimneys*, this method of articulation is overt; the general narrative is interspersed with a set of short stories; these, though they may appear to break up the flow of the plot and stay the climax, in fact form one thread leading towards it. In *The River*—perhaps the most rambling and least well organised of the series—while all the episodes are formally submerged in a single narrative, the total effect is a bit disjointed: each adventure is finely rounded off in itself, but the final *dénouement* owes little to what has happened in most of them. *A Stranger* and *An Enemy* are simpler in structure and follow a unified story line; even so they are punctuated by a number of major pauses. This common element in the structure of the books may hardly seem worth commenting on; but the skill with which Mrs Boston weaves the short rhythms of individual episodes into the much longer rhythm of the main plot deserves remark in itself; and I am convinced that, for younger children, an important virtue of her books is that because of this structure they lend themselves so easily to being read aloud.

The Children and *The Chimneys* are most alike in structure, in plot, in texture—and are also the most technically daring of the books. At the beginning of *The Children of Green Knowe* (1954), a small boy, Toseland (his name, not very mercifully, is soon shortened to Tolly) goes to stay for the Christmas holidays with his great-grandmother, Mrs Oldknow, as his father and stepmother (whose unsympathetic character is very neatly indicated by the fact that *she* calls him Toto) live in Burma. A note of strangeness and impending mystery is immediately struck: for Tolly arrives at Green Knowe at night, by boat—the house looks like Noah's Ark in the fenland floods which lap about the doorway. And his great-grandmother, whom he has never met before, is very old—though not frighteningly so, as he had anticipated.

On the very night of his coming Mrs Oldknow's conversation is full of clues that the house is invested with special properties, and when Tolly wakes the following morning he hears a strange creaking in his room—'it seemed to him that the (rocking) horse had just that minute stopped rocking'. At breakfast he notices a painting of three children and two ladies, hanging over the mantelpiece: they are seventeenth-century ancestors of his, who also lived in the house. As the book progresses the present and the past begin to entwine. As he explores the house, stables and gardens Tolly finds relics which once belonged to the children in the picture. He hears laughter and unseen feet.

34

When he plays an imaginary game of hide-and-seek a twig, cut into a perfect T, is placed lightly on his head. In the meantime, in the evenings Mrs Oldknow tells him stories about Linnet, Toby and Alexander, how Toby was nearly drowned on his horse, Feste, going to fetch the doctor on a stormy night, how Alexander was appointed to sing in a *Masque* before Charles II and won the royal gift of a flute. In the most delicate but formal counterpoint, as Mrs Oldknow brings the children to life in her bedtime stories, so they come alive to Tolly as he plays around the house—at first only hearing them, then catching a glimpse of them in the mirror in the hall, then joining in their games and talking with them. The climax of the book arrives when Tolly, wearing Toby's coat, goes down to the stables early on Christmas morning. The ghost horse Feste eats an apple from his pocket. A little later he is given a fieldmouse by Linnet. Now 'he no longer feared that the children would disappear and leave him, and perhaps never come back. He felt that they were like brothers and sisters who come and go, but there is no need for worry: they are sure to come home again'.

The plot of *The Children* is poetic and fragile: timidly handled it might become static and uneventful; treated too brashly it would simply fail to compel attention and belief. Mrs Boston succeeds in creating momentum and suspense partly through skilful transitions; but more because she never lets her readers think of her theme as a fantasy, as a voyage into the unreal. Meeting a make-believe ghost is ultimately a banal experience; contact with the genuine article, on the other hand, is intrinsically exciting. Linnet, Toby and Alexander are presented with robust conviction—there is none of that playful facetiousness which trivialises Oscar Wilde's Canterville Ghost. As a result their slow materialisation, which has the effect of merging the present and the past, is neither scaring nor arbitrary, has none of the irritating tricksiness of a clever conjuring act, but is breathtakingly interesting.

Nevertheless, compared with *The Children of Green Knowe, The Chimneys of Green Knowe* (1958) is much more ingeniously and strongly constructed. Tolly is again staying with his great-grandmother for the holidays; and again Mrs Oldknow's stories and his own adventures in the house and garden act as dual incantations to summon up children from the past. This time the stories are evoked by an old patchwork quilt which Mrs Oldknow is repairing: they introduce us to the Oldknow family at the end of the eighteenth century.

In *The Chimneys*, however, Mrs Oldknow's tales are less like exquisite vignettes. Instead they tell the history of the family, ending up with a tremendous conflagration in which all but the ancient Norman backbone of the house is burnt down, and the wicked butler and the family jewels both disappear, never to be seen again. As the counterpoint to Mrs Oldknow's narrative, Tolly not only meets Susan and Jacob, and discovers a secret tunnel; at one moment he actually takes a dramatic part in the events that happened a hundred and sixty years earlier. *And* he finds the lost jewels—thus saving Mrs Oldknow from having to sell the picture of

Linnet, Toby and Alexander, for which she has been offered a very tempting price.

For neatness of design, it would be difficult to surpass *The Chimneys*; it reminds one of those Russian dolls—there is plot within plot within plot. Yet it is not simply in its more brilliantly engineered structure that it differs from *The Children*. Susan and Jacob, kind Captain Oldknow and his flighty wife, and all the rest of the Regency characters are livelier, more fetching, and less entirely good than Linnet and her family. Susan and Jacob, in particular, are masterly conceptions: Susan is blind, and chained in inactivity by the assiduous feather-bedding of Nurse Softly and the contempt of her mother; Jacob is a Negro slave boy, bought by Captain Oldknow, rather against his better judgement, in the West Indies, and given over to Susan as servant-protector-companion. The passages in which Jacob with a delightful blend of resource-fulness, courage and discerning gaiety releases Susan from a narrow bondage of darkness are most imaginative and moving. Also, the incidents in *The Chimneys* are more exciting, build up greater suspense. Jacob's rescue of Susan in the fire, bringing her safely to ground through the network of sizzling chimneys, is very exciting indeed, and gives a foretaste of Mrs Boston's talents simply as story-teller, talents which are put to more central use in the later books.

But this comparison is a little unfair to *The Children*. For if *The Chimneys* is undoubtedly the jollier, livelier affair, this is partly because in it Mrs Boston is painting a picture of Regency

England and does justice to its odd mixture of grace, humanity, sturdiness, raffishness and squalor: a sophisticated combination of Zoffany, Bewick, Rowlandson and Sir Thomas Lawrence. Whereas she sees the seventeenth century with the eyes of Van Dyck, hears it with the ears of Purcell, and feels it a little in the terms of Traherne's *Centuries of Meditations*: hence the intense, refined, exquisitely beautiful and remote mood of the core of *The Children*; and hence, too, the gravity underlying the characters of Linnet, Toby and Alexander—a gravity never far removed from exaltation and tears. Not immediately apparent, the evocation of a period of history turns out to be a basic dimension of both books. In the ease with which she carries her historical knowledge, and in her penetration of the mood, the look, the very smell of an age, Mrs Boston reminds one most of Virginia Woolf's virtuoso performances in *Orlando*.

Another theme which eventually gains the centre of one's attention in these books, is the relationship between Tolly and his great-grandmother, and with it, the flowering of Tolly's personality and imagination. The growing understanding and affection between the two is never treated obtrusively, but runs, a homely and stabilising current, throughout the books. Because of their great disparity in age there are no vicissitudes: Mrs Oldknow teases, prompts and appreciates Tolly, Tolly occupies, entertains and squires Mrs Oldknow. It is an ideal, easy-going companionship which never seems to go stale.

Having established the pattern in *The Children*

and *The Chimneys* one presumes it would have been possible for Mrs Boston to continue indefinitely a series in which Tolly and Mrs Oldknow discover and make friends with children from every period of Green Knowe's ample past. But she was not satisfied to repeat this successful formula, and in *The River at Green Knowe* (1959) she struck out in a different direction, sweeping away her old cast of characters (except the house itself), and dethroning adventures into time past from a central position, as well as giving up the device of stories within the story. Now Maud Biggin and her friend, Sybilla Bun, have rented Green Knowe for the summer; they invite three children—Ida, Dr Biggin's niece, and Oskar and Ping, two 'displaced children'—to come for the holidays. While Dr Biggin writes a book about primeval giants and Miss Bun cooks, the children, left to amuse themselves, explore the river. Their final adventures, in which they find a living giant, persuade him to join a circus, leave one of his enormous teeth on the lawn—which Dr Biggin accepts as genuine—and take Dr Biggin to see their giant's act—which she regards as an imposture—tie the book neatly together. But for the rest it straggles and twists, sometimes sluggish but shimmering, sometimes swift and turbulent, very much like the river round which it is written.

If *The River* is less skilful in plot and less consistent in mood than its predecessors, there are plenty of compensations. Biggin and Bun are a couple of comic eccentrics portrayed with a mixture of farce and affection—a sort of blend of *Decline and Fall* and *Cranford*. Dr Biggin's oscillation between scientific credulity and scientific scepticism is touched in with gleeful irony; Miss Bun's ruling passion for food is preposterous, even silly and obvious, but becomes funny through the immense verve with which it is pursued. How completely and joyously she lives in a world all clam chowder and puff pastry! The children, too, are very rewarding. Oskar, a Polish boy whose father was shot by the Russians, is tall and truculent, rather commonplace in spite of his determined spirit, and a good foil for Ping, a Chinese boy whose subtlety of physique is matched by his decorous courtesy of manners and shining imagination. Ida, tiny but self-possessed, bosses the trio, occasionally with a touch of feminine shrewishness, more often through sheer ebullience. And besides all their adventures, which include ghost flying-horses, an owl-haunted ruined house, a bus-conductor turned hermit, as well as the giant, the book is rich with the glitter of dragonflies, the rustle of long grass, the clear images of clouds in the water, the scents of night, the ladened pleasures of an English river landscape. Really the book is about the country delights of summer: picnics, bathing parties and deliciously idle afternoons in the sun. As a lady once said of a Constable painting: 'how fresh, how dewy, how exhilarating!'

Ping captured one's heart in *The River*. It was a pleasure—and no surprise—when he reappeared in Mrs Boston's next book *A Stranger at Green Knowe* (1961).* The outline of the main plot of *A Stranger*

* Awarded the Library Association Carnegie Medal.

is extremely simple: fate brings Hanno, an escaped gorilla, and Ping—who have already confronted each other in the London zoo—to Green Knowe, now once again inhabited by Mrs Oldknow. Ping keeps Hanno's presence a secret, even from Mrs Oldknow. But of course the authorities are searching for Hanno, and Ping, despite all his efforts, cannot conceal the clues to his whereabouts. The book ends on an appropriately tragic but triumphant note: Hanno, a creature built for majestic freedom, is not recaptured but shot.

The opening of the book is a very remarkable piece of writing, for Mrs Boston has the daring to describe Hanno's life as a small gorilla in the forests of the Congo. Her account of the family life of gorillas, while it is lucid and clearly based on careful research, has a poetic insight which is very rare indeed. It is far away from the sentimentalities of *Black Beauty*, the dubious humanising of animals of *The Wind in the Willows* or even the vigorous but coarse depiction of animal character in Masefield's *Reynard*, and can only be compared to the superb animal poems of D. H. Lawrence and Leconte de Lisle. It also has a most important technical function for it establishes the titanic quality of her hero, the gorilla, and of his natural surroundings; so that when Hanno is caged in the concrete of the zoo one feels more than a perfunctory humanitarian sympathy for him, and his few days' final freedom are worth the price of death.

Behind the suspense generated by Ping's perilous friendship with Hanno and its inevitably tragic ending are at least two major themes. One is the conflict in Ping's loyalties. In order to keep Hanno concealed and fed he has to indulge in many ill-mannered subterfuges, all the more painful to him because Mrs Oldknow is not only his hostess but a person he comes to love deeply. Yet he cannot divulge Hanno's presence in the thicket to her: this would be to involve her in an impossible and horrible quandary and lead, willy nilly, to Hanno's betrayal. Ping emerges as a person of great integrity and moral—as well as physical—courage.

The other theme is 'displaced persons'. Ping falls in love with Hanno because of his enormous dignity —and perhaps because he is *not* a human being. But the roots of his quick sympathy and under-standing lie in the affinity of their experience of life. Both have been tugged away from their homes; both have lived in loneliness and in the harsh indifference of institutions; both have had to face the prospect of an unmeaning future. This affinity is made quite explicit by Mrs Boston; and the book gains much of its fierce power from her attack on the inhumanity of trapping animals, of zoos, and of transit camps. It is not an undiscrim-inating onslaught; she makes it clear that captivity is crueller to some animals than others; and her portrait of the headkeeper of the zoo is subtle and balanced: ruefully, and with much tenderness, he accepts the convention of the menagerie. On the other hand there is a satisfying contemptuous venom in her depiction of a big game hunter and of the moronic crowds who shuffle past the bars at Regent's Park.

A Stranger is an exotic book; Green Knowe becomes a place of bamboo thickets, tropical downpours, pervaded by the musky smell of the gorilla, mingling strangely with the scent of roses. The quality of Englishness, so strong in her other books, is subdued here. And the historic past is of no importance at all. Even the house plays only a minor part in the proceedings.

Not so in *An Enemy at Green Knowe* (1964): here the house once more provides the motive force of the drama, for it is under a threat—a threat of the most dangerous and sinister kind. Mrs Oldknow is in residence; and staying with her for the end of the summer holidays are Tolly and Ping. Scarcely has she had time to tell the children of one of the more bizarre episodes in the history of the house, in which a terrifying alchemist was invited there to tutor a young and sickly Oldknow, when pat comes a letter from a Miss Melanie D. Powers (Ph.D. Geneva) asking if she can come to visit Green Knowe as she is interested in Doctor Wolfgang Vogel and what happened to his library. Both children know that they can expect adventures. But what occurs exceeds their (and any assiduous reader of Mrs Boston's) expectations. First they see an extraordinarily evil face in a magic Persian mirror. Then the face, now glossed over with a nauseously genteel expression, comes to call in the person of Miss Powers. Odiously nosey, pushing and persistent from the start, Miss Powers makes it clear that she shall be relentless in her pursuit of Dr Vogel's lost library of occult books. Unrelenting—and she is a witch. First she attempts to cast a spell on Mrs

Oldknow, and nearly succeeds in tricking her into selling Green Knowe. Failing, she lays siege to the house, visiting it with a series of increasingly loathsome plagues in the hope of scaring Mrs Oldknow into submission. But the children keep an eye on her and her nefarious projects with the aid of the magic mirror, and manage to avert each successive danger. They also find one of Dr Vogel's ancient volumes, a manuscript of *The Ten Powers of Moses*. And greatly daring, they pay a visit to Miss Powers' squalid den. With aid of *The Ten Powers of Moses*, the tattered pages of which are pieced together by Mr Pope, a medieval scholar who by good fortune lives in the annexe at Green Knowe, Miss Powers' last and most diabolical attempt on Green Knowe—a disembodied hand begins to pull down the rooftree and gable end—is scotched. And with the information culled in their reconnoitre of her hide-out, the children exorcise Miss Powers' own personal demon.

An Enemy at Green Knowe is not a leisurely or comfortable book; the analogy of a country train does not fit it so very well. Miss Powers is no second-rate witch, grotesque but incompetent, able to send a few agreeable tremors up and down the spine, but not to assault the citadel of virtue. On the contrary she is a most potently malign creature, fully armed to pervert the natural order; and so, as calamity after calamity is unleashed against Green Knowe, anxiety about the outcome rushes the reader from scene to scene. Mrs Boston's other stories could be characterised as 'discovery' plots; like flowers they unfold a petal at a time; essentially they are harmonious. *An Enemy* is a book dominated by conflict; it is full of brimstone turmoil. Mrs Oldknow, who in the other books seems imperturbable, is thoroughly rattled—at one moment she almost seems ready to concede her defeat. The children are so busy in countering Miss Powers' strokes, that they hardly have time to enjoy anything. It is an anguished autumn in which pleasure parties are turned to desperate contests of good and evil.

To say that *An Enemy* is no bigger than its main plot would be wrong. The magic mirror for instance takes up the thread of one of Mrs Boston's favourite themes—time. There is a fine counterpoint in the relations between Mrs Oldknow and her brood. Mrs Oldknow realises the risks the children are running, and hates to put their bodies or souls in jeopardy; the children, for their part, are determined to protect her; and all are indomitable in their loyalty to the house. Yet these matters are essentially embellishments to the striking pattern of the drama. The book *is* overshadowed by the baleful sneering countenance of Miss Powers, and when sunlight streaks its last pages the reader blinks in surprise.

Mrs Boston's latest book, *The Castle of Yew* (1965), written for the Bodley Head Acorn Library, represents her only deliberate attempt to write for younger children; it is very much shorter than her other books; it has a much slighter plot. Although set in the garden of the Manor, it is outside the 'canon' of the Green Knowe books.

The first reaction to *The Castle of Yew* of any

reader who has followed carefully the course of Mrs Boston's development as a writer, is probably a mixture of bewilderment, surprise and unwilling disappointment. After the rich, agitating dramas of *A Stranger* and *An Enemy*, with their mastery of narrative suspense, their strong colouring, and their insistence upon moral problems, the tiny, dainty quality of *The Castle of Yew* is, to say the least, unexpected. The adventures of a small boy who enters a strange garden owned by a strange old woman, who admonishes him with the strange words 'You can go anywhere you want, if you really want to', turn out to be tepid, timid stuff, compared with the experiences that Tolly and his friends come up against. Joseph finds a chess set cut in yew bushes. The castles, though they are diminutive, have real doors, windows and battlements. Encouraged by the old woman's words, he decides to go into a castle and shrinks to the appropriate size. He enters a fine green hall. Shortly after, another older boy arrives.

The adventures of the boys all derive from their change in scale. The castle is attacked by a moorhen, to them a dangerous dragon with a frightening big beak, and besieged by a black cat with eyes like round windows and claws as big as hayforks. With great ingenuity Joseph uses the contents of his pockets, matches, a sparkler and a firework to frighten the intruders away. He even manages to repel the mischievous attack of a squirrel—gorilla size—with an elastic band. Finally, though they have enjoyed themselves enormously the boys decide it is time to stop playing but are perplexed as to how to regain their normal scale. By a cunning transformation scene of their own devising they are metamorphosed back to their normal stature and make their way gaily out of the garden.

Delicate, slight, neither highly inventive nor original in its main lines, still *The Castle of Yew* is more rewarding than might appear at first sight. The character of the elder boy, Robin, is charmingly sketched. He sees the whole thing in terms of Arthurian romance and with delightful bombast introduces himself to Joseph as 'Sir Valiant of Cornwall', and appoints him to be his page. All his talk has a delightful, mock heroic ring about it: ' "We'll have dinner upstairs . . . Can you eat a whole nut? That stack of buttercup petals in the corner is the plates. We throw them away after using. It's the modern way. Follow me, page".' With its slightly quizzical tone—which the boys themselves adopt—and with its sparkling and poetic perception of a miniature world, the book offers its older readers some of the same sort of pleasure that Pope provides in *The Rape of the Lock*. The young children for whom it is specifically designed must find it both exciting and tantalising.

For the critic the book has a special value. The very fact that here, for the first time, he is conscious that Mrs Boston is addressing a juvenile audience, highlights the ability of the other books to invoke the interest of grown-ups directly, their maturity and depth of interest. It also exhibits how sure her craftsmanship has become. For though her plot may be thin and flavourless to adult appetites— especially when compared with the other books—

47

the story remains immensely fresh and pleasurable to read. It makes one realise how close, how sensitive, how Tennysonian in its detailed but imaginative accuracy, is her gaze and her diction.

III. Mysteries

'About half an hour later, when tea was over, and they had risen from the table, Mrs Oldknow offered to lead the way upstairs to see the rest of the house. Miss Powers was standing with her back to the table, her hands clasped behind her, lingering to look at the picture over the fireplace, when Tolly, happening to dart back unexpectedly to pick up a pencil that had dropped from his pocket, saw one of the little French cakes move, jerkily, as if a mouse were pulling it. Then it slid over the side of the plate and twitched its way across the table and into the twiddling fingers held ready for it behind Miss Powers' back.'

In this discreet and deadpan way, Mrs Boston introduces us to the black arts of Miss Powers, arch-villain of *An Enemy at Green Knowe*. That nimble cake sends a pleasant shudder down the spine, and gives the reader an agreeable foretaste of the frightening mysteries to come.

Dr Johnson did not much care for the books of Mrs Trimmer; they were too mealy-mouthed and full of morals. On the other hand he fully approved of fairy tales and nursery rhymes for children, for they fed a child's imagination with what it needed, good strong meat. I think Johnson would have been a bit in two minds about Mrs Boston's stories. While he would have loved the French cakes, the magic mirrors, the wicked butlers, the giants, the hermits, the gypsies, the fires, the winged horses, the ghosts, the strong streak of fantasy in her books, he might have been slightly nonplussed at the great refinement with which she handles these themes: he might have thought the fantasy too filigree and fanciful.

If this were the case, he would have been wrong. Probably Mrs Boston's books do owe a part of their popularity amongst children to the fact that they deal with subjects that children (and grown-ups) have always found exciting. But their real claim to distinction and originality lies precisely in the great imaginative tact and delicacy which she brings to traditional situations and topics. Some of the episodes in the books are in themselves hackneyed: the bus-conductor turned hermit in *The River* is one of a thousand descendants of Robinson Crusoe; the episode in the same book where Oskar shrinks to the size of a mouse, and the whole action of *The Castle of Yew*, are no more than variations on a theme in *Gulliver's Travels* and *Alice in Wonderland*; the kernel of *A Stranger* has provided the material for a hundred books—one is inevitably reminded of Mowgli. Yet in her hands they attain a new, highly individual and exciting meaning. That Mrs Boston deals in mysterious matters is not remarkable; what is remarkable is that she does such justice to their mysteriousness.

The mistake which so many writers make in treating of witches, or ghosts, or giants, is to portray them in so blatantly marvellous a manner that though they provide fine images for the imagination to feed on, they do nothing to rouse a child's intellectual curiosity. However delightful fairy tales are, they suffer from one very serious failing; they are incredible. Too often they depend on an entire divorce between fantasy and fact. As a result they tend to teach us to separate the life of reality from the life of the imagination, to the ultimate impoverishment of both. It is the singular virtue of Mrs Boston's books, that so far from opposing the strange and the ordinary, the things which we find it hard to believe and the things which we take for granted, they weave the commonplace and the magical so closely together that each is touched with, and transfigured by, something of the essential quality of the other. It is impossible to shrug off her ghosts as figments of an exotic imagination; they are far too substantial and challenging for that. At the same time she invests so everyday a happening as an afternoon bathe in the river with a curiously powerful air of the miraculous: it becomes an utterly unique—and consequently highly incredible—event.

Thus, throughout her books, Mrs Boston keeps her readers in a delightfully tantalising state of mind, quite unable to decide whether or not to believe in all the mysteries with which she confronts them. Does Tolly really hear the rocking horse creaking, or does he merely hear it with his inner ear because he wants to hear it? Does the ghost horse, Feste, take the sugar lumps which Tolly leaves in his stall, or have they disappeared into the teacup of Boggis, the gardener, as Mrs Oldknow mischievously suggests? Did Linnet give Tolly a real fieldmouse, or was he only playing make-believe with the wooden one which he pulls out of his pocket to show young Percy Boggis, all the time?

Did Ping, Oskar and Ida really meet a giant called Terak, or was Dr Biggin, in spite of the preposterous illogicality of her position, right in thinking the performing giant at the fair a clever fraud? Did Tolly really see that nimble cake flitter into Miss Powers' hand when he bent forward to pick up his pencil, or did he merely think he saw it?

Sometimes one is swayed towards incredulity. When Oskar does his shrinking act one gets thoroughly doubtful. In common experience young boys simply don't dwindle to the size of a mouse, for no better reason than that they have a fancy to do so. And yet Ida's sudden outburst of ill-temper and bullying jealousy at pigmy Oskar, ensconced in Ping's pocket, sways one back again. It is so natural, so right a reaction. On the other hand, throughout those desperate days when Green Knowe is beleaguered one fully believes in the malevolent magic of Melanie Powers; yet at the end of the book on reflection one cannot help wondering whether all along she was no more than the pathetic, slightly crazy, but quite harmless woman who finally slinks away on the penultimate page, and whether all the plagues might not have some other less terrible explanation.

Perhaps this helps to make clear what I mean by saying that Mrs Boston does justice to the mysteriousness of mysteries. It is one of her great strengths that she never attempts to explain a mystery away: how one hates it when a perfectly good ghost turns out to be no more than an escaped lunatic, or the after-effects of eating too many peppermint creams at bedtime, or one of incorrigible uncle Theobald's ingenious practical jokes. At the same time she never forces her reader to believe more than he wishes to. Tolly's commerce with Alexander, Toby and Linnet, or with Susan and Jacob, may be no more than the heated imaginings of a very lonely boy, seeking out playmates. The fact that Mrs Oldknow encourages him in this game does not upset the interpretation. For Tolly himself is not always sure whether or not she too sees the children. And if she does, it may be that she too has been lonely, she too has a sharp imagination.

Yet though Mrs Boston does not enforce her belief in mysteries upon us, all the time she is tempting, persuading, by the deftest technical means coming nearer to cajoling us into assenting to the reality of her ghosts, her gorillas, her giants. For her, it would seem, one of the great vices is incredulity, disrespect for mysteries . . . and though Dr Biggin may be right, Mrs Boston pokes a good deal of fun at her. If she is adamant in any one thing, it is that we should take the possibility of the existence of ghosts, the possibility that somewhere in the world there are still men ten cubits high, the possibility that human beings can deliberately encompass evil by magic, seriously. It might seem easy to sum this up by saying that she has little trust in contemporary rationalism, that she believes most scientists have missed the essential point of living, that for her, the life of the imagination lies at the centre of human existence. But this does her some injustice. The temper of her books is not anti-rationalistic and though she makes fun of scientists and of 'Ph.D.s' it is certainly light-hearted satire and

53

no more than 'Ph.D.s', at least, deserve. Moreover she is certainly not a protagonist of indiscriminate credulity. If we take her books at their face value they ask us not to believe in any old thing but precisely to ponder certain problems which human beings have always found baffling.

Thus the stories have a strongly philosophical undercurrent—which may seem rather inappropriate in view of their primary audience. Yet the books themselves help us to remember that children are often much more involved than grown-ups in trying to answer the most difficult questions that life evokes and do so much more freshly and vivaciously. Grown-ups tend to sweep the problem of evil under the carpet; grown-ups tend to sweep the problem of human personality and the survival of bodily death under the carpet; grown-ups tend to sweep the problem of time past and time future and their relation to time present under the carpet; grown-ups tend to sweep the problem of illusion and reality under the carpet; grown-ups tend to sweep gorillas under the carpet: grown-ups have large carpets and powerful brooms. Children are less cavalier in dealing with such puzzles. Indeed they seem to enjoy them, as exercises both for their nascent powers of logic and for their ability to experience drama vicariously.

Certainly all the children who come to Green Knowe have something of a philosophical cast of mind—even the belligerent and extrovert Oskar. Ping is the most deeply thoughtful and it is typical of him and of the mood of the books that he pauses to ponder wicked Dr Vogel's aphorism: 'What's thought cannot be unthought'. Ping's ability to chew upon experience, to wrestle with it, to try to extort a meaning from it is a leading trait in his character. Without it the whole adventure with Hanno, the gorilla, would be impossible. For Ping does not appreciate Hanno's intense nobility of character, or the poignancy of his predicament, simply by intuition; he thinks these matters out. In doing so he helps the reader to discern and admit the inner life of Hanno and consequently gives what might otherwise be a fantastic tale great credibility and a more pondered meaning.

Tolly too is an unusually responsive and imaginative child. When Mrs Oldknow tells him about blind Susan he immediately attempts to understand the experience of blindness from the inside and spends the following morning blindfolded on the lawn, capturing for himself somebody else's world. In the same way he does not simply accept the existence and nature of ghosts as a fact. He entertains the possibility that he may only be dreaming; he does not presume that because he sees Alexander, Toby, and Linnet that quite automatically Mrs Oldknow will; he learns slowly and a little painfully, perhaps, to have confidence in the wayward and different world of apparitions; so to speak, he works out the rules by which they exist. It is probably the thoughtful responsiveness of Tolly and Ping, Ida and Oskar, to all the surprises of Green Knowe, their desire to comprehend, to take nothing for granted but to see all that they do and all that happens to them as some kind of whole that, as much as anything, provoke in the reader a similar

honesty, patience, and receptiveness. It is their discussion, for instance, of the magic mirror which
sparks off a whole chain of musing about both time
and the oddness of a reflected world in the reader's
mind.

To say that Mrs Boston's books have a philosophical undercurrent might suggest that they are
tedious and stodgy. This is far from the case.
Though the texture of the books is consistently
thoughtful, though the children are always probing
and analysing the mysteries, they do so in a casual
and buoyant way. There is no hint of dry and
systematic academic discourse. A much more
pertinent criticism of Mrs Boston's penchant for
mysteries is that she sometimes asks us to take
rather trivial and unrewarding mysteries a little too
seriously. Perhaps it is the fact that grown-ups
cannot easily get excited about the possible existence
of giants which, as much as the rather loose con-
struction of the book, makes *The River* the least
rewarding of the stories. One must be careful, however; though giants may not be a live issue for
adults, they may be very genuine mysteries for
children. Moreover they are a good way of
approaching what is a permanently fascinating
theme: how our human scale orders everything in
our experience of nature.

And the series of interrelated themes to which
Mrs Boston most frequently returns is a fundamental one. What may appear a rather fanciful pre-
occupation with ghosts is only a brilliant way of
dramatising a more deep-seated concern with time
and human personality. A recurring motif of the

books is the discovery of some lost relic of the past, a key, a signboard for Feste's stable, the model of the good ship 'Woodpecker' which Captain Oldknow gave to Susan. Always these relics stir the life of the past into activity; they behave as messengers travelling into the present, telling of old deeds, old emotions, old plots, old villainies, old loves, which because they have once happened must exist forever, and prompting Mrs Oldknow and her brood to investigate and rediscover them. Put in comparatively formal terms, Mrs Boston seems to be saying that all human actions are incomplete in time, that for every act there remains a residue of unfilled intention which stretches out beyond the event itself. In her boldest treatment of time she goes further than this. In *The Chimneys* time flows in all directions and Tolly does not merely meet with the past in a sort of no-man's-land of time, but steps back into the eighteenth century to come to the aid of Fred Boggis.

Of course this fluidity of time enables Mrs Boston to devise exciting stories, full of surprising twists and turns; and it is possible to argue that she is less concerned to convince her readers than to amaze and delight them. Certainly it gives her wonderful opportunities to explore the daily life of the past in a particularly intimate and sensuous way. It also means that her books have a rich variety of content as she skips from the twentieth into the eighteenth century or the seventeenth century or prehistoric times and back again. It enables her, too, to approach death—a stumbling block which most children's writers either evade or trip over with deplorable clumsiness—with sensitivity and realism. The passage in *The Children* when Tolly finds Toby's sword and asks Mrs Oldknow why Toby no longer wants it, and Mrs Oldknow divulges that Alexander, Toby and Linnet all died in the Great Plague is most moving and tender. ' "After all," she said, "it sounds very sad to say they all died, but it didn't really make so much difference. I expect the old grandmother soon found out they were still here".'

Well, there are people (we must admit) who will find this aspect of Mrs Boston's work intolerably fey. But such people are likely in general to find her irritatingly 'poetic'. It is not that the strange happenings usurp the whole of each book. On the contrary, the mysteries are made to form part of the everyday life of her characters, who go on eating, sleeping, making jokes, and feeling occasionally out of sorts and sour, in spite of them. Rather it is that with remarkable consistency, she portrays the whole of human existence as potentially mysterious, with ghosts and witches as merely some of the most amazing items. To illustrate just how alert she is to the fundamentally perplexing and exciting attributes of the world in which we all—and children most readily—live, how much a feeling for the strange, the elusive, the mysterious is part of the basic idiom of her style, I can do no better than quote from a passage chosen at random: Tolly unpacking his Christmas stocking.

'There was a flashlight refill from Boggis. A telescope from his father. In his bedroom he could only use the wrong end but it was almost better. He looked at the rocking-horse and it would have fitted into a matchbox. He found Toby's sword, the right size for a chaffinch. The chaffinch was hard to find, no bigger than a ladybird. In the looking-glass opposite his bed he saw himself as if across a wide valley, miles and miles away. And if the things in the room were small, their doubles in the doll's house had reached vanishing point.'

This is not a virtuoso passage. There are dozens of moments in the books when Mrs Boston tinctures common things with the magic of sharp perception expressed through startling images.

Though it may put off people who are dull and matter-of-fact in mind, who believe that children should be served a leaden broth of fictionalised juvenile sociology, who, in a word, are twentieth-century Gradgrinds, it must be said that there are no books in which a ghost or a giant is more naturally and tremendously at home, than in Mrs Boston's stories of Green Knowe.

IV. Friends and Enemies

Suppose our great-grandparents had been suddenly enabled to step forward a hundred years no doubt they would be duly surprised by all the things which we would expect and hope them to marvel at: moon-probes, antibiotics, television sets, nylon stockings. But we forget that they might be a good deal more astonished at the programmes on television than at the sets themselves, at the bold tracts of leg that women now show than at how those legs are clad. The short time it takes to cross the Atlantic would be much less shocking to them than the short time it now takes to preach a sermon.

The fact is that new manners have transformed our world as completely and abruptly as the new technology. Of all the metamorphoses in modes of behaviour and taste perhaps none is more extraordinary than the change which has been wrought in our appetite for moral discourse. In one of the best passages in his masterpiece, *Portrait of an Age*, G. M. Young has described the Victorian hunger for moral instruction and edification: it was a passion which permeated every art form and even adorned tradesmen's cards and hotel menus. That bold voracity seems to have dwindled away to the most discreet and genteel nibbling. The impression one gains from contemporary literature is that nowadays there is much more rejoicing over the ninety-nine sheep who go permanently astray than over the one silly lamb that somehow manages to get found again.

No department of Victorian literature was more

deplorably and relentlessly edifying than books for children. These terms may seem unfairly harsh. They are not intended to suggest that children's books cannot properly be concerned with moral problems; on the contrary it would be my contention that they should, and that it is their unreadiness to be so that robs so many modern children's books of any really satisfying meatiness. What is objectionable in Victorian literature for children is not its concern with values, manners, standards of behaviour, but the crude repetition with which it imposes what are usually jejune and superficial precepts. Even so psychologically sensitive a writer as Charlotte M. Yonge could not resist creating priggish heroes and banging home her lessons with sledge-hammer blows when a light tap or two would have more than sufficed.

Critics have been quick to notice the closeness of Mrs Boston's books to the great classics of Victorian children's literature. Indeed there is something old-fashioned and substantial about the very format of her books: the paper is thick, white, smooth to the touch; the margins are handsome, the type pleasantly large—but not at all infantile— and the inking rich and black; the text is charmingly embellished with printers' ornaments. The illustrations, too, add to the impression of nostalgic and leisurely solidity. Peter Boston has that uncanny and very Victorian ability to marry his drawings, particularly his modest vignettes, to the mood of his mother's text; in *The Chimneys* they achieve something of the freshness, honesty, humour and yeoman beauty of Bewick, in *The Children* they evoke memories of the delicacy of a Wenceslaus Hollar engraving or a piece of Stuart lacework.

Perhaps the most obviously old-fashioned characteristic of the stories themselves is Mrs Boston's habit of making her happy endings especially festive by dishing out extra lollipops to her heroes. Thus in *The Children* Tolly is given a pony and told that in future he shall go to the choir school at nearby Greatchurch instead of returning to Miss Spudd's unappetising academy. The triumphant finale of *An Enemy* is made yet more delightfully triumphant by the sudden arrival of Ping's long lost father at Green Knowe in company with his great friend, Mr Oldknow. It is surely only a mean and griping critic who would object to such fortuitous but lavish acts of generosity on the part of an author.

The books reflect Mrs Boston's Victorian upbringing in other subtler and more important ways. She does not hesitate to give vent to her indignation at the callous and ignorant attitude of the common crowd who file past Hanno in the zoo or the almost equally stupid remarks which the villagers make about him in the local shop. Here one sees her fearless evangelical conscience at work: her account of the big game hunter, Major Blair, is mercilessly reproachful. Nor does she hesitate to give vent to her awe and delight in the face of natural beauty. Victorian writers were much too robust in their appreciation of the frank splendours of things like mountains and sunsets to worry very much if they gushed and gave way to 'purple passageing' in describing them. Like them Mrs

Boston is ready to respond with an opulent style to opulent effects; here is one of her pieces of homage to a sunset: 'The heron was flapping home across the islands to the heronry, the swans climbed up on to the bank and there raised their pointed wings high like Seraphim before folding themselves into white curves for sleep. The river was a lake of glassy fire, because the sunset was still in the sky, but over the roof of Green Knowe pale green daylight still hung with the evening star there again, and the rapt flight of bats.'

The Victorians were perhaps less inhibited than we are in enjoying grand and gaudy natural effects because they were so much more deeply versed than we are in natural history. Ruskin's most high-flown paragraphs were always rooted in minute knowledge and intensely careful observation; he could let his pen go because he knew what he was writing about. So too can Mrs Boston. And like Victorian naturalists she has a tremendous appreciation for the tiny details of flowers, insect and bird life, with which they balanced their worship of the sublime. She belongs to a generation that was still brought up on the natural history books of people like Philip Gosse, J. G. Wood and F. O. Morris; she must still have been a girl when those marvellously precise, humane and elegant books of J. H. Fabre began to appear in English: her intimate understanding of and joy in such everyday country creatures as fieldmice and water beetles is strongly reminiscent of the great French naturalist.

We are often taught, nowadays, to think of the Victorians as being far from certain and optimistic in their values. There is some truth in this. Yet if one considers so typical a figure as William Barnes, the Dorsetshire poet, one cannot deny the extraordinarily settled and convinced quality of his belief in natural beauty. Nor can one miss the fact that this belief is a part of a total complex of stable and deeply held personal values. In much the same way Mrs Boston's conviction of the reality and value of beauty is part of a larger confidence she has in her own standards of right and wrong, her identification of a moral order. And perhaps it is the sheer firmness of her moral judgements which more than anything else is ultimately responsible for imparting an air of the old-fashioned, of the Victorian, to her stories.

I am well aware that such epithets might easily be taken to be uncomplimentary. This is not my intention. They must certainly not be taken to imply that the books simply evade modern times or trade on old-world charm. Motor bikes, noisy youths, the six o'clock news on the wireless, are a part of life at Green Knowe as well as Elizabethan fireplaces and Regency dining chairs. The children are a good deal less old-fashioned than was little Paul Dombey; they can think in terms of rockets and displaced persons along with the rest of us; even in her style Mrs Boston is totally unarchaic— for instance in *The Castle of Yew* she describes the bumble bees as flying past 'droning like helicopters'.

Nor, in using these terms and in emphasising the clarity of Mrs Boston's values, do I wish to suggest her books are mere repositories of moral maxims, that she is ponderously and persistently didactic in the manner of Mrs Sherwood or *Eric; or Little by Little*. On the contrary her stories are singularly free from any attempt to preach, admonish or even inform. No nice, neat, moral conclusions lurk insidiously just beneath the surface waiting for priggish little readers to fish them out. If she does allow virtue to be rewarded, the rewards are subtle and suitable and not doled out in automatic largesse. And if her characters are good and lovable they are so in ways far from conventional. They are not sententious copy-book kids who infallibly sport the correct mixture of beautiful manners, pious intentions, dutiful acts and wise reflections; there is nothing milk-and-water or meretricious about them. Ultimately the books are powerfully morally persuasive—and this is one index of their quality. But that they are so is because Mrs Boston desists entirely from any direct attempt to sway her readers by argument or exhortation and relies instead on the intrinsic validity and force of her values as they are embodied in action and in the feelings of her characters. To use a commonplace but apt term she is an unusually committed writer, who leaves us in little doubt about the nature of her commitments.

One of the foremost of these (and one which must particularly delight her younger readers) is a commitment to recognising and respecting children as independent, complete, intelligent and capable beings. This respect is not based on an idealised and unreal estimate of children. It is true that Mrs Boston depicts them as much more good than bad

—but this is not to idealise them. In fact she is careful not to hide their weaknesses and faults. There are moments when Tolly is dependent as well as disgruntled, when Oskar sulks, when Ida nags. Mrs Boston does not gloss over the foolhardiness of Ping, Oskar and Ida's adventuring upon the river when it is in full flood; nor does she pretend that Ping's concealment of Hanno is, in every sense, wise. She lets her children make mistakes—and perhaps it is this which makes them so credible and *un*-insipid.

Her attitude is mirrored in the attitudes of the grown-ups in her books. The nicest thing about Dr Biggin is that she doesn't interfere, she isn't forever prying, questioning, cajoling, adjuring, popping her inept adult fingers into the children's private pies. She opposes Miss Bun's tendency to fuss with dry, unflappable humour: her reaction to the children's escapade in the flood is typical in its gruff common sense. No reproaches, no grumbles, no admonitions for the future—just ' "I should have thought you'd had a first-class adventure and nobody any the worse".'

It is clear that Mrs Boston thoroughly approves Dr Biggin's readiness to let the children be what they are. By contrast she heaps coals of contempt on those characters who do not respect her children, from Major Blair to Miss Powers. One more black mark is chalked up against the Major for referring curtly to Ping as 'that boy'; Miss Powers from the first is shown to be unspeakably odious, but she is at her most disgusting when she tries to chum up with the children, riding roughshod over their

66

natural dignity and reticence and demonstrating that she has none of her own:

' "The front entrance is the usual and the shortest way," said her hostess. "Tolly, please show Miss Powers out that way. So far she has only come through the back. Good-bye, Miss Powers."
"This way, please," said Tolly, polite and businesslike. But as soon as she was alone with him ... the visitor became arch and condescending. She bent down and poked Tolly in the ribs. "Poker face! I don't like children to be stiff with me. Let's play rabbits. Rabbits always follow the known track. Come on, race me!" Away she went at full speed ...'

Needless to say Tolly does not follow her.

The respect which Dr Biggin, the head keeper of the zoo and, in particular, Mrs Oldknow show for the children is of fundamental importance for it is reciprocated by the children themselves: and on this mutual agreement not to invade each other's privacy, to trust each other's judgement, to appreciate each other's feelings, is based the peculiarly warm and solid friendship and affection between the children and the 'good' grown-ups, which is perhaps the most impressive and moving theme of the books as a whole. One of the most depressing things about many children's books (Arthur Ransome's *Swallows and Amazons* series is a good example) is that they insist on children and adults being at loggerheads, each inhabiting mutually exclusive worlds of thought and action. In Mrs

Boston's books they share each other's jokes, pleasures, flights of fancy. What could be more charming and right than the present that Tolly chooses to give Mrs Oldknow for Christmas? He buys it at the local nursery garden:

' "Have you a rose in a tiny pot that only grows three inches high?"

"Yessir. Rosa minimissimasir. Three andsix-sixpencesir."

"Does it smell?"

"Yessir, they saysosir; if your noseissmall-enoughsir".'

In much the same way as she insists on respect between people Mrs Boston is committed to a respect and veneration for nature. She rejects whole-heartedly the notions that people may be 'manipulated' and that nature may be 'mastered'; her children explore trees and fields and the river, on the look-out for mysteries and surprises, but they are never wanton or senselessly destructive. The value she puts on harmony and amity with natural things pervades all the books but perhaps is most overt in *A Stranger* with its superb picture of the great equatorial forest in which the gorillas are so magnificently at home, its derision of the false environment of the zoo, its worship for and love of Hanno himself.

Friendship and concord between the old and the young; between the present and the past; between human beings and animals; between man and nature: these may seem rather an obvious and dull, if worthy, set of values. But in Mrs Boston they are not. Partly because of the passion with which she maintains them: the world she conjures up is very coherent—made so by her style and her moral sensibility—so that whether she is writing about a tuft of grass or the death of Hanno she strikes a fine balance between sympathy and objectivity. But more because she is able to show how important, how essential these values are, because she shows them in a world in which they are threatened.

In the earlier books the threats are not so very serious, but in *A Stranger* and *An Enemy* they are very grave indeed. Mere common sense would demand that Ping tell Mrs Oldknow about Hanno, and Mrs Oldknow tell the authorities; moreover, Ping's decision to keep his secret costs Hanno his life. Here faith and love triumph over common sense—but at a sad cost.

In *An Enemy* the values by which Mrs Boston—and her *alter ego*, Mrs Oldknow—stand are yet more directly assaulted; this is what, perhaps, makes it the most difficult as well as the most exciting of the books. Of course we may see Miss Powers as nothing more than a witch, given all the proper accoutrements and a dash of malice to boot, who simply behaves as any witch should. But surely she stands for more, for all those people who not only live by greed and self indulgence, who disregard all scruples to attain their ends, but are so lacking in natural reverence that they are prepared to wrest nature from its proper course, to create distortion and perversity to minister to their insatiable desire for power.

So fierce is Miss Powers' onslaught that Mrs Oldknow does falter in her confidence, does, in her fear for the safety of Tolly and Ping, contemplate leaving the witch in possession at Green Knowe. Faced with the alternatives of selling her house or putting these children's lives in jeopardy, well she might. It is the proper measure of the value that Mrs Boston puts upon beauty and fitness and of her scorn for impiety, that she makes Mrs Oldknow, with the help of the children, fight it out.

It was not simply Milton's artistry but a grandeur in his soul that made him depict Satan as so majestic a Prince of darkness. It says the last word for Mrs Boston that she makes Miss Powers the most tremendous witch.

Yew Hall, Faber and Faber, 1954.

The Children of Green Knowe Illustrated by Peter Boston. Faber and Faber, 1954.

The Chimneys of Green Knowe Illustrated by Peter Boston. Faber and Faber, 1958.

The River at Green Knowe Illustrated by Peter Boston. Faber and Faber, 1959.

*A Stranger at Green Knowe Illustrated by Peter Boston. Faber and Faber, 1961.

An Enemy at Green Knowe Illustrated by Peter Boston. Faber and Faber, 1964.

The Castle of Yew Illustrated by Margery Gill. Bodley Head, 1965.

AMERICAN EDITIONS

The Children of Green Knowe Harcourt, Brace & World, Inc. 1955.

Treasure of Green Knowe (*The Chimneys of Green Knowe*) Harcourt, Brace & World, Inc. 1958.

The River at Green Knowe Harcourt, Brace & World, Inc. 1959.

A Stranger at Green Knowe Harcourt, Brace & World, Inc. 1961.

An Enemy at Green Knowe Harcourt, Brace & World, Inc. 1964.

The Castle of Yew Harcourt, Brace & World, Inc. 1965

*Awarded the Library Association Carnegie Medal for 1961.